SOLITARY STILLNESS

SOLITARY STILLNESS

Kiriti Sengupta

HAWAKAL PUBLISHERS

Published by: **Hawakal Publishers**, 185, Kali Temple Road,
Nimta, Calcutta 700049, India.

Website: www.hawakal.com
Contact: info@hawakal.com

First edition: August, 2017

Second edition: May, 2018

Printed and bound at Thomson Press (India) Ltd,
New Delhi

Cover concept and design: Joyeeta Bose

ISBN-13: 978-93-87883-08-6 (2nd Edition)
Price: INR 150/- [USD 7.00]

Critical Acclaim for Kiriti Sengupta

With his master strokes, Sengupta offers an all-pervasive analysis of the microcosm, his seemingly nonchalant style being the most powerful weapon to demolish our long-cherished views about human life: the claustrophobic existence in the City of Joy as depicted in "The Bengali Phenomenon"; the suffering of Christ in the time of crucifixion as written in "Expressions"; and the appalling lightlessness when shadows grow longer as portrayed in "Illumination." Sengupta extends the metaphor of the book's title in some of the poems, emphasizing the essential loneliness of our existence when we speak to ourselves in prose or verse...we are compelled to realize how lonely we are yet how rich in poetry, and [*Solitary Stillness*] is a preparation of the voyage to meet the "infinite" with a poetic brush.

—***World Literature Today***

Kiriti Sengupta does not restrict himself to non-issues and subjective musings. His sensibility encompasses themes on religious, cultural, environmental issues as well as subjects on agony, amour, and alienation. The blending of the prose and free verse with effortless ease in this book speaks volume of the poet's skill in the use of English-language. The poet dexterously juggles the two forms, discernibly an innovative style. *Solitary Stillness* wafts a cadence of stillness when one is through with it. There is an inherent silence in most of the poems but it is loud enough to be resonated in the heart of those who have an ear for quietude.

—***Dissident Voice***

It is wisdom that is the essence of any aphorism. It is not only the mixing of Eastern and Western literary traditions but also mixing of prose and poetry, the mixing of Indian and Western cultures, and the mixing of expression and silence...Silence works insidiously in Sengupta's poems, working its way where words are absent and making spaces for loudness of thought, hypnotism of interpretations and, perhaps, in self-deprecating way, overratedness...[*Solitary Stillness*] speaks of the stillness of solitude. It is a morsel that can be masticated for long.

—*Cafe Dissensus*

Sengupta's poetry has always had the motif of spirituality woven into them, and in [*Solitary Stillness*], the wise maturity has seen through death too much: the pieces are not morbid, but they are solemn, and [Sengupta] has shown restraint in this regard.

—*Red Fez Magazine*

To my friend, the scholar Kaushik Acharya

FOREWORD: Shadows Receiving...

Kiriti Sengupta issues another missal to awaken the world to its imminent horizon! Life is rarely what it seems, and the larger picture sneaks in over the smaller prints ["*Smaller waves failed to erase the footprints!*" as written in "The Shoreside"]. We are creatures of habit, and the silence is a way to shear our minds of these habits and their creed. We tire of ourselves sometimes, and the world wears us completely out with its demands and faux wisdom. Poetry, even *Poetry*, can seep into unreason and the noisome rather than seek to avert the hypnotic hysteria of world matters.

In *Solitary Stillness*, the new chapbook from Sengupta now in your hands, we are shown what it is to shun the world for one's personal pleasure and leisure. Yet Sengupta does not entirely rid himself of the world. He frequently affirms it in poems such as "High Rise" and "In Conversation With…" in which he shows how careful protection encourages isolation and loss of risk, the great teacher. A poet cannot and should not keep silent in times of trouble, but a poet especially needs quiet moments to reflect. Sengupta has written numerous works over the years, and I have studied several of them in detail. I even wrote reviews and the foreword to *The Earthen Flute* as well as published *Reflections on Salvation*. Readers familiar with these works will find this verse collection most kindred with *Reflections on Salvation* and *The Earthen Flute*.

I tell the reader this because this poetry collection is strikingly different yet similar to previous works but has retained certain qualities from them. For one, the verses are a mish-mash of syntactically similar devices. The terse paragraph that offers glimpses of thought is reminiscent of *Reflections on Salvation*. Dare we ask what the purpose of these tediously interpreted yet ripe "flash" paragraphs is? We are not being told the whole truth, only segments of it, as if to balance our thinking a certain way. Tip us to the edge of truth? Sengupta is capable. *Flash Wisdom* as a genre has prospects to become a world movement if promoted by fans and readers alike. I wrote a flash wisdom collection, published by Hawakal Publishers, earlier this year and the topic of approach was different, but the overall purpose was the same as Sengupta's *Reflections*. *Flash Wisdom* as a genre attempts to make use of the ancient paths while showing how the folly of humankind distorts the simple truth. Truth is also boldly complex. All religions offer great, inspiring paradoxes that have been pondered for centuries. Jesus tells a wealthy individual to give half of his wealth to the poor. Wouldn't that make the poor, wealthy? Why is this gentleman condemned to Hell for not sacrificing his fortune? Let's think abstractly as both Sengupta and I have done. This isn't a financial message delivered. Jesus also referred to the kingdom of Heaven as something immaterial. It is within you, not something you can retrieve or earn. It is rather something you get glimpses of through sustained consciousness.

Wisdom, that highly sought yet abundantly ignored prospect, appears as a questioning and also a unification of ancient wisdom with modern concern — the praise of folly is widened to include the crass materialism and strife riches often bring. We are goofy children who don't know what is best for us and yet we strive to take risks and render ourselves absolved after development. I am sure Sengupta and I are not the only ones wondering why the words of Christ are used to condemn those who command less or who suffer from conditions they cannot help.

The poems resemble *The Earthen Flute* in their existential drama and earthiness. The poem "[Re]Formation," for instance, can lead a perceptive reader to understand how and why his work has faced transformation. Changes sneak up in various forms and are already with him through the process of his next collection. They are rendered "parcel of your constitution." This clever piece of humor is also serious in scope. Each work re-writes and re-interprets the previous ones because the change was hiding in sufferance all along!

As Sengupta noted in a recent interview, "Poets are self-motivated souls." We will write even if Mr. Hyde emerges from our words! There is nothing greater to a poet than the catharsis of raw emotion through the interchange of words on the page. The poem "Illumination" is an imaginative delicacy for the mind because it is "equivocal." Dark is the absence of light and yet shadows can only exist with light. In the poem, the shadows walk with the bodies attached to them thus precipitating their walk. Is an illumination perhaps something predestined, but will only strike when the mind is receptive? Is wisdom inherent in the natural world, inherent and immutable? Why then is everything in flux? Is a poem a moment similar to the one described in "Illumination?"

"Rolling Stone," "The Pillars of Soil," and "Tournesols" each refer to water in a diverse sense of symbolism. "Tournesols" creates a sense of resurrection through Vincent van Gogh. The poet remarks that his wish was that there was "water in the vase" of sunflowers painted by van Gogh. Rain and monsoon waters are seen as refreshing and symbolic of hope in the alternate two poems. Water is universally seen as cleansing, symbolic of both blessing and redemption. Perhaps if van Gogh could have seen his dry sunflowers offered hope, he would have lived longer.

"Expressions" exults in dialectical logic and synthesizes with the mystery of the Cross. The reader is left to ponder the validity of expression as a medium of prayer. Prayer means not keeping silent in moments of despair and agony. Expression is protest and it becomes one with the world in vigilance. The written word is powerful and irrevocable yet, "Write to Eat" laughs at the condition poetry faces — the poem seemingly addresses the Muse, the flippant La Belle di sans Merci who both tantalizes and damns — in the sense that the poet is expected to consider his own work. No, *critics* are the plumbers of the language of damnation!

These poems unite culture and language in a variety of word games and descriptive allusions. There is the timeless question of when to keep silent. There are political questions riddling the terse writings and there is a sense of edgy humor and advice. After reading the collection, you are left with a feeling of buoyant dream. I recommend revisiting *Solitary Stillness* a few times to understand its purpose.

Dustin Pickering
Editor-in-Chief, *Harbinger Asylum*
July 27th 2017
Houston, Texas

Introduction

Poetry is essentially equivocal. It can be loud and exciting; it can be declaratory, or read as an epigram; and it can also be unadorned and prosaic. Nonetheless, poetry induces stillness to its readers. When I say "stillness" I don't refer it to as worldly immobility. Poetry bears the impeccable quality of being meditative, and meditation leads to stillness.

India is witnessing much of communal and political pandemonium lately. People often inquire about a poet's stance in these turbulent times. Honestly, on such testing moments, I would rather ask them, "Can you remember the day you read poetry of late?"

We have protesting poets all across the world, and we also have poets who become silent in times of unrest. They aren't the ones feigning indifference to the situation. They are rather the sensitive souls who absorb much of the prevailing anarchy, suffer from inside, and put down their thoughts in other ways around. There are times when clamor is best avoided.

I won't say much on the poems included in this collection. A poem should speak for itself and deserves to be interpreted in several ways. All I can say is I've consciously written on subjects I have not tried before in my earlier books. Poets are loners, no doubt! I've explored the joy of uniqueness, and I hope readers will greet the serenity in the poems I have gathered in *Solitary Stillness*.

Kiriti Sengupta
July 17, 2017
Calcutta

In all the lines I have written,
and all the words I have said;

I wish I was blessed with restraint!

Contents

ome t
mory la
rp and I
byways
ced about
He thou
little drun
tions of h
er sudd
Sha
er the
eminis
drifted
d and a
mplica
ould nc
said Lart
up from h
mably.

The Pilgrimage

"Pipiray pak uthe moribar tore…"
Phullara says, "The ants grow wings to fetch
death…"

Fire is clearly not the cause,
however their flight, the pilgrimage!

Note: The proverbial saying, "The ants grow wings to fetch death,"
has its reference with *Chandimangalkavya* by Mukundaram
Chakraborty. Phullara is the wife of Kalketu, one of the
protagonists of the medieval Bengali text. It is believed, ignoring
inevitable death, ants fly into fire due to ignorance.

The Bengali Phenomenon

Trust me, we are essentially nonchalant
and waste time...
Jubilation ahoy!

It took ages to savor the ecstasy
until Lapierre released his *City of Joy*!

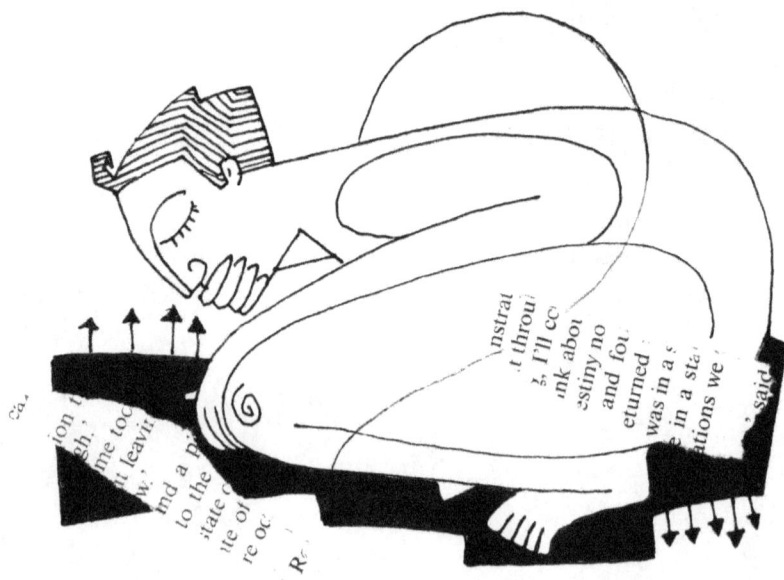

Quietude and Loneliness

For god's sake, don't take silence for granted!
It is loud, hypnotizing and over-rated.
It has a spiritual world charm attached to it;
you never know if it will declare you dead.

And then you can see the resurrected spirit
approaching your stillness
and challenging the world
to leave you alone!

Tournesols

after Vincent van Gogh

Make them alive, I said,
give them the sun and a parrot,
if you think right.

At-least some gay yellow shine…
Wish he had listened to me

while he painted the sunflowers on canvas.

Life would not have stilled
had there been water in the vase.

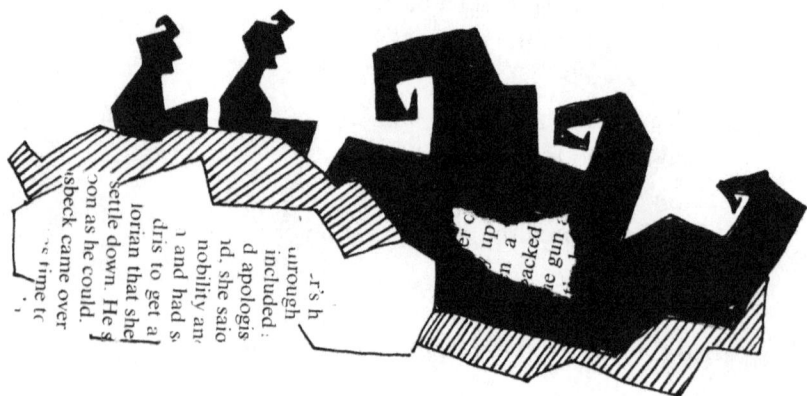

r's h
urough
included :
d apologis
nd, she said
nobility an
1 and had s
dris to get a
lorian that she
settle down. He s
oon as he could.
usbeck came over
s time to

The Shoreside

It was an early winter evening;
my friend, Bitan, and I went to the beach.
He urged me to sit on the boulders along the shoreside.
A wide spread of mountainous rocks lying on the coastal sand,
no sign of erosion — sharp, edgy and difficult to walk on.

I sat on a stone for some time...
It was exciting to see the water reaching us
and foaming below our legs;
we did not want to soak the salt.

The boulders were loosely bound

Small waves came to merge with the sand,
they failed to lather much.

Smaller waves failed to erase the footprints!

Large waves arrived to hit the rocks,
they filled up the space existing in between.

Larger waves appeared — abrupt...
The sea sprinkled on our dry skin.

Manhattan Skyline

Not bothered
if the world thought in more than one way
on Dylan's winning of the Nobel prize

I won't justify his long silence either
or if he was rude
as the Swedish Academy failed to reach him by phone

Readers read when Dylan told the British paper:
"Amazing, incredible!"

No comments
Better I keep silent
and continue to look at the skyline

The *Manhattan Skyline*

Here lies an artist

Here lies a merger between two men:
A man who sings
and a painter who strikes through the concrete lane

A breathtakingly vast sky tinted with yellow
A bridge marked the horizon
and below mellowed the water in pale sorrow

No landscape but infinite met the brush
mind stilled you bet
while "traveling the back roads, freeborn style"

Note: *Manhattan Skyline* is one of the paintings by Bob Dylan,
exhibited recently (November 5, 2016) at the Halcyon Gallery in
New Bond Street, London. Dylan has written a preface to the
exhibition catalog, which says that his works have "something to
do with the American landscape" while "staying out of the
mainstream and traveling the back roads, freeborn style."

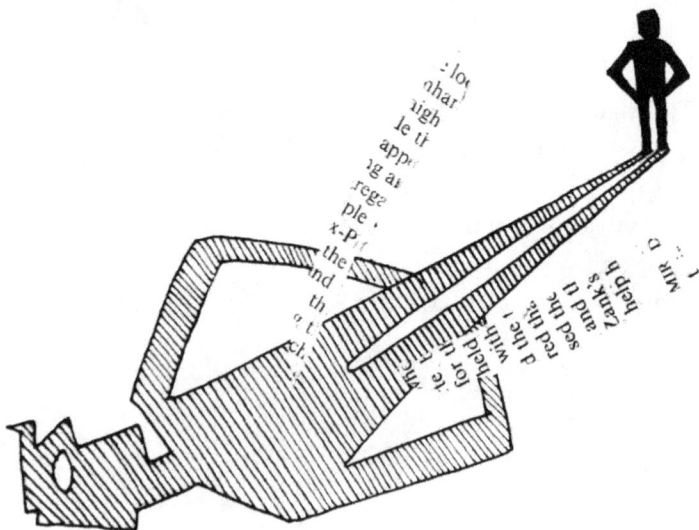

Illumination

We were walking down the solitary lane
from the light to the dark end
We two men saw twin selves
but not in flesh

The shadows

They emerged from their mortal frames
thinner
but didn't hesitate to grow longer
and even surpassed
as we went ahead
Our shadows cherished
every bit of the lightlessness

until a sudden gush of glow bathed us

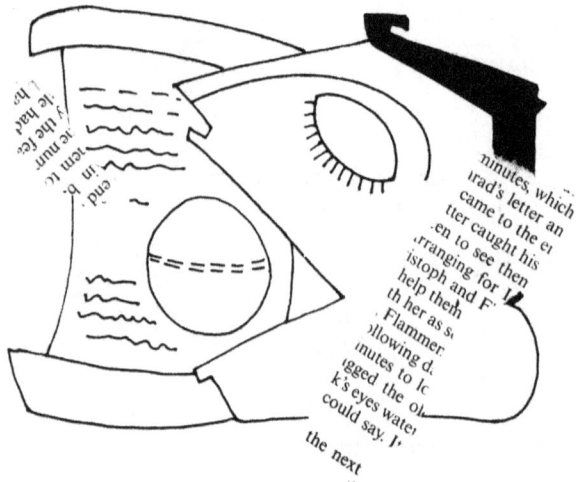

Poetry, Cricket and Two Neighborhood Countries

Securing an exclusive passport for my upcoming Bangladesh trip has been easy. It is my neighborhood country; we speak in the same language: Bangla. They respect their native tongue more than we do in India, let alone Kolkata.

Trust me, securing the visa has been easier!

I have been consistent in praising their poetry for six months approximately; I picked the major ones — living.

I also chose a few who I found enterprising … I promised I would translate a few into English.

They nominated my name for an award. They considered me a deserving poet and I was happy.

Last week India fought against Bangladesh, it was an international cricket tournament. They were defeated … Oh hell! We bad-mouthed … They were hell-bent and spoke highly about their sportsman spirit

We said how well we played; it was probably the umpire who was held responsible as he missed out on a few leg-before-wickets, they said.

Poetry took a backseat; they don't buy my appreciations anymore!

A few intellectuals from my city called them a circumcised race, but then it was nothing major; an age-old tradition, existing on or before the Partition. Culture upholds religion more than the history and British Empire.

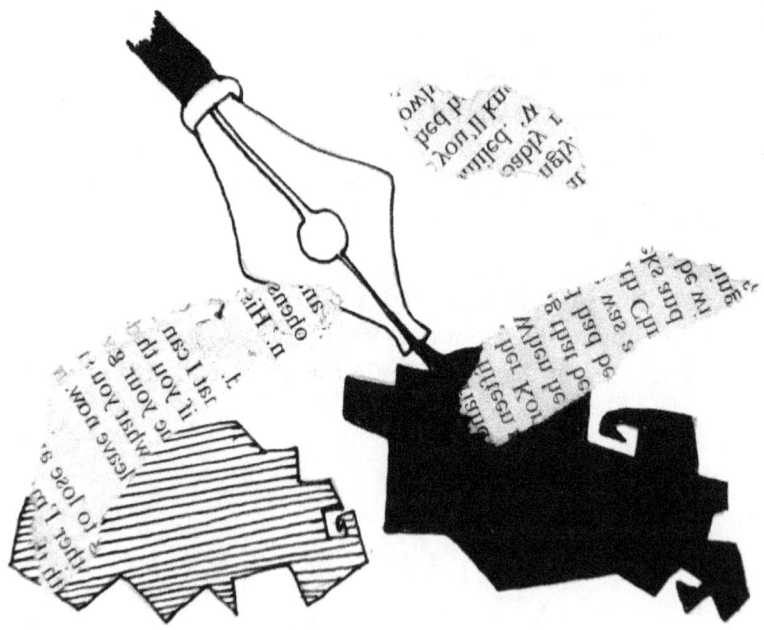

Write to Eat

Did you mean regurgitation? I'm afraid of vomiting.
Let the sac receive the food; I'll let my gut absorb its
vital nutrients. The world dislikes a vomiting neonate!

I lose words as I write; my pen loses ink with every
word it puts down, and are you asking me to withdraw
the lines I sketched? The ink has set on the paper; the
pot can't be refilled with scribbles. Do I now surrender
my pen?

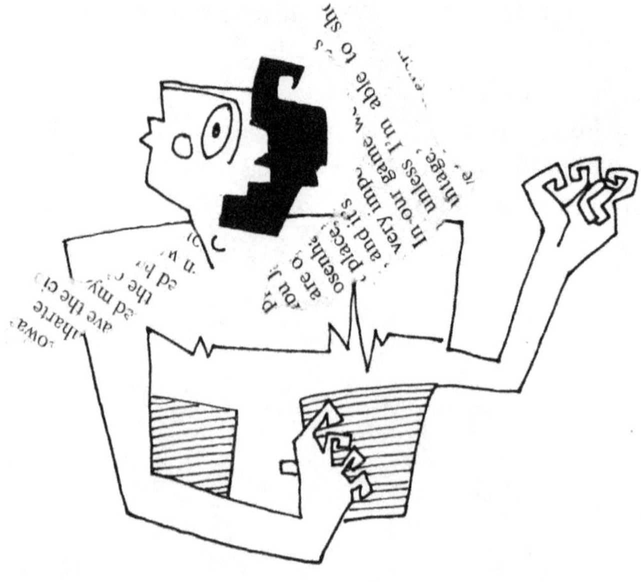

(Re)Formation

You either have a regular or irregular pulse. But then, the irregular could play in a regular rhythm, or you might have irregularly irregular pulse. In all such conditions men don't cease to breathe and live. A deviation from normalcy is not necessarily pathology! You never know when your body accepts the changes and makes them a parcel of your constitution.

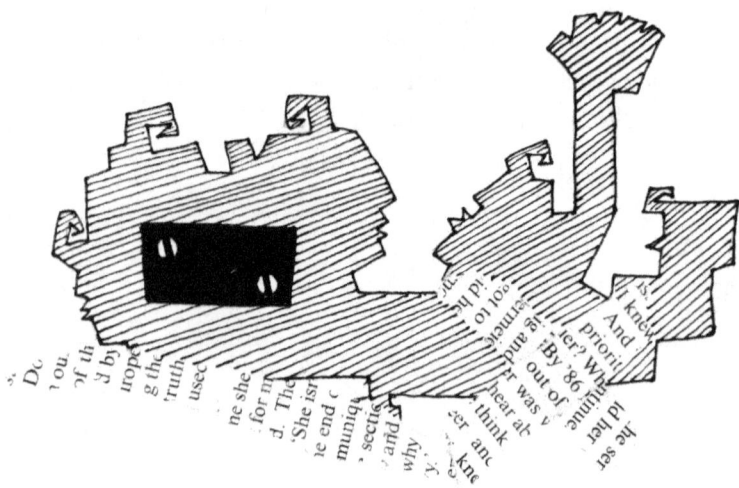

Expressions

A protest lacks in our humble submission,
otherwise we would have named it
an appeal to the authority.
An appeal is devoid of
our being buried underground,

or else we would have called it
prayer to the Lord.

Did Jesus keep silent
when they nailed him to the cross?

Love Story

Why does my photographer friend
ask the models to avoid greasepaint?

I think
the camera reciprocates a mirror

The mirror makes an impression
and reveals the concealment
of flaws

The camera mocks the disguise
and celebrates light

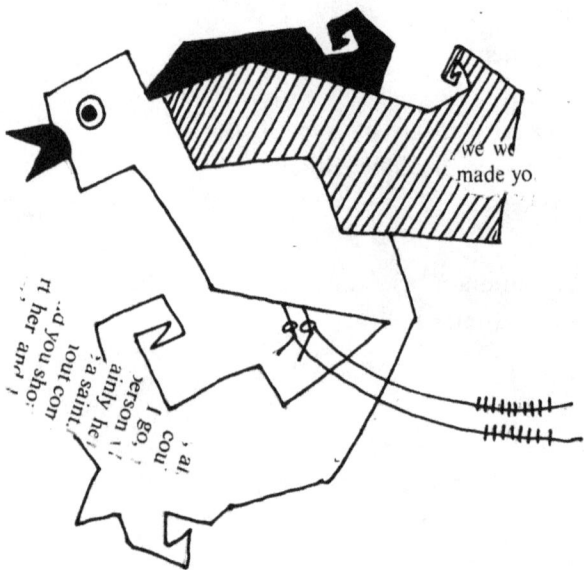

High Rise

Look at the egg-baskets around
you will find them of several designs
and varied shape
The most common being the ones
which look like a cage

No matter how tall your claim is
no matter how cool your lawn breathes

birds no longer fly high

Like the eggs
we love to keep the birds
safe

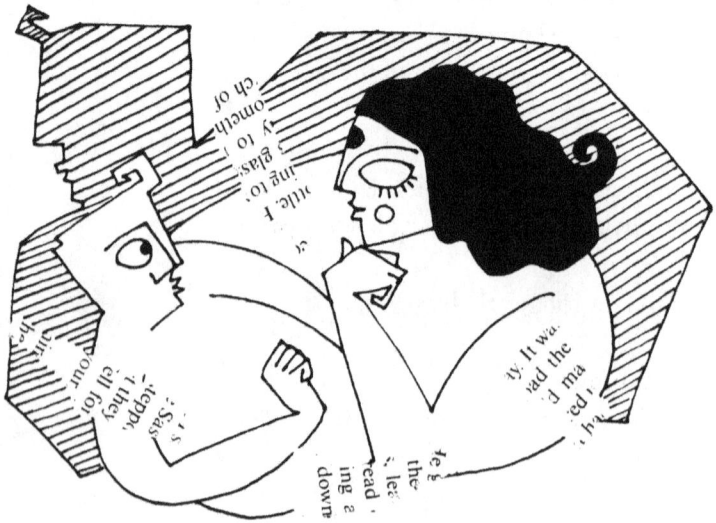

Patriarchy

mithye [lie] *tumi* [u] *dos* [ten] *pipilika* [ant]

Ma, you taught me the easy formula
so I could spell the word correctly,
every-time I wrote
lieutenant.
But, instead of the ten and ant

you could have asked me
to write tenant.

Was this because you always
detested a rented accommodation?
Was this because, other than
the house you owned and bragged about,

all along you lived a life where
Baba remained the chief, and you
his subordinate?

In Conversation with...

I thoroughly enjoyed horror movies, but, honestly, I was scared of ghosts! Nonetheless, the first-day-first-show was a must, and if by any chance I failed, I cursed the people around. On every successful attempt the film affected our sleep.

If I had to go to the washroom I used to call momma, "Keep awake until I come back." She remained watchful. After marriage it has been my wife always.

I now have arrived to an understanding. I no longer seek company. To my utter bewilderment if the ghost succeeds to appear, I've decided to offer it a chair first, and then I'll plead, "Take a seat and relax! Let us share our stories..."

The nights were never so long before.

the back
Ulrike b
three n
t the n
gun a
e sou
men.
er, and

OPPE
e The
ing

own b
ity centre, h
er street she s
ithdrew it an
r mother
It says

Approach

My wife has been consistently advising me to quit smoking; she raised her voice first as she celebrated my 40th birthday. She thinks 40-plus men form a high-risk-group for cardiac arrest. I didn't tell her, I heard my heart first on the same day!

Rapid pulse ... ambiguous pain around the jaw ... and a sense of breathlessness... I had fine tremor, my eyes reddened, and I stood before a large mirror to see if I was looking good as usual. I can tell you, there was a bunch of weird feelings. But honestly, I did not think of my son!

I thought about my wife; I wanted to figure out the pain she might have to live with, and I was equally curious to anticipate if she would tell my mom, "Your son never listened to me!"

I was consoling myself; I was sure my wife would not easily give up, she would rather live her life to address the promises I failed to live up to. But then, I got a strange feeling: Would my wife take care of the books I wrote?

Rolling Stone

It's not that I have never fallen in love with another woman post-marriage. I appreciate women and beauty like other men of my age, and as I used to in my heydays! It's not that I'm committed to myself for not building an extramarital affair being a so-called faithful husband. But, what do I expect from the other woman? Is this only about being intimate, or passing time?

On every such occasion of nurturing the idea of a second relationship, I now ask myself: Will she offer me a glass of water when I return after a long day? Will she cook for me? Will she take care of my ailing health?

And, will she be interested in accompanying me to the doctor?

She is not, and she has never been my wife, after all.

The pre-monsoon showers relief,
but only temporarily.
The earth fails to dissipate heat
enough to sustain its composure.

And, the sky won't allow the clouds
for long. They will rather find
another summer
to captivate and tantalize.

The monsoon is remembered,
it is yet to arrive!

gatew
an fifty
side
heart
afety c
men e
undled t
ring that
e door w
e couldn',
ld certain'

d the
ig an
to L
you
is yo
next
ten
ders
ole
nc

Table Manners

Sayan, a friend, said, "Use your manners!" I ate *Biryani* with my hand in a posh restaurant. He was visibly upset, "You are spoiling my reputation, and must respect the ambiance of the place you are dining in." I kept silence for a while.

Sayan had ordered Chinese noodles, which he took by a spoon and fork. The waiter rushed to our table, and asked him hesitatingly, "Would you prefer chopsticks, Sir?"

Instead of answering the boy, Sayan looked at me — shocked! I cheered him up, "Take it easy! Foods are generally culture-specific, but then, there are several other etiquettes that keep the aura alive."

The Pillars of Soil

"There are several elephants up in the sky," a friend giggled, I can remember, when we were studying in the first grade of our elementary school. I believed in her words until I learned the science of rain ... how the clouds collide and melt into drops ... how the trees aid in rainfall, etc. By then we had read about the amazing legends on *Mia Tansen*, the great maestro, and how he fetched shower while performing *Megh Malhar* in the royal court of *Akbar*, the *Mughal* emperor.

On my way to an old-age home

56

I witnessed the cloudburst once more:

The trees alongside the expressway
were listening to the music of precipitation
with their heads bent down.

As if the wood was enjoying
tender care after a long-long time.

As if the trees were paying attention
to the instructions sent from the sky.

They were probably being told
the world would need another maestro
who could sing for the seasoned flesh;

who ran their roots deep into the ground,
and the ones who walked the earth—
the pillars of soil.

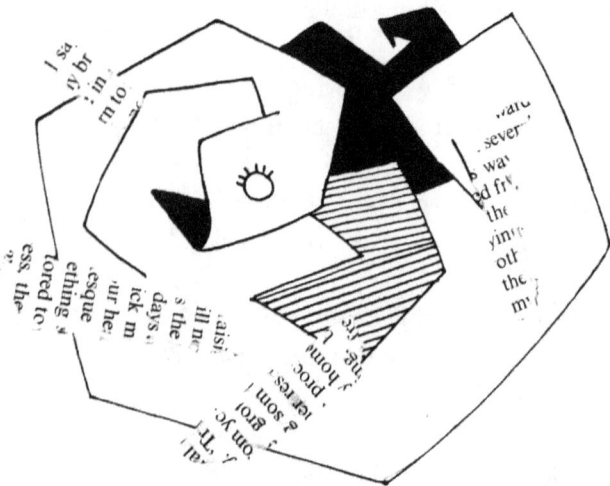

Where Do Old Birds Go to Die?

I've no idea, but here is a question:
How long does a bird live to be called old?

I've seen careless crows die from being
electrocuted, although I'm not sure
if they are the ones the birdwatchers look up to.

I've found dead birds in the cage,
Ramu*da*, my neighbor has built,
facing his house — a public showcase!

Every time I see an abandoned nest
of the weaver bird in a Bengali household,
I appreciate the perseverance of the bird,
who has been loyal to its intricate home.

Honestly, I've never been close to the trees
where birds build their house;

I've never been intimate with the leaves,
fishes, fruits, or the pests
a bird eats...

I'm not aware where birds hide
when they are unwell, but
I can say, birds heal themselves,

and die solitary
amidst the quiet flora — unnoticed!

Note: The title of the poem came from a chapter of Arundhati
Roy's fiction novel, *The Ministry of Utmost Happiness*.

Acknowledgements

Thankful to Helen Ivory at *Ink Sweat and Tears*, Duane
Vorhees at *Duane's Poetree*, and Johnny R.Olson at *Mad Swirl*,
who accepted and published a few of the poems on their
webzine and blog.

Heartfelt thanks to Marc Paltrineri for offering me
suggestions and edits.

I'm indebted to the following people: K Satchidanandan,
Sanjukta Dasgupta, Debapriya Bhattacharyya, Dustin
Pickering, Casey Dorman, Thachom Poyil Rajeevan, Seb
Doubinsky, Koushik Sen, among others.

Dustin, you deserve special mention as you are the one who
named my book, *Solitary Stillness*.

Critical Acclaim for Kiriti Sengupta

Kiriti Sengupta's poems are powered by a sense of profound irony that lends them an unmistakable contemporary touch. He remains deeply Bengali even while choosing to write in English, giving his poems a bilingual sensibility.

—*K Satchidanandan*

Solitary Stillness traverses a new poetic path. This chapbook is indeed a turning point in the career of Kiriti Sengupta. In this new venture Sengupta juxtaposes prose and verse, subjective musings and macro issues; [these] poems are remarkably well-wrought, exuding both sense and sensibility in the use of the English language and the poetic content.

—*Sanjukta Dasgupta*

As with many of Sengupta's past collections, *Solitary Stillness* is exceptional because of the manner in which the poetry captures those moments of experience that reveal truth. From the particularities of the rocks and sea and waves and foam in "The Shoreside," to the effect of watching one's shadow as one walks from light to dark and light again in "Illumination," the emphasis is upon seeing and experiencing, the limits of which are also explored in the poem "Pillars of Soil," which interprets the fall of rain from the framework of the cultural metaphors learned in childhood. The descriptions and insights are exquisite.

—*Casey Dorman*
Editor, *Lost Coast Review*

Solitary Stillness is a nice collection of colorful vignettes, which reveal all the subtleties of life seen through the prism of an acute poetic eye.

—*Seb Doubinsky*

Kiriti Sengupta has taken up the challenge of expressing the inexpressible, solitude and stillness. Meditative, reflective, and receptive, the poems in this collection exemplify the art of catching the real disguised as the unreal. A brilliant book.

—*Thachom Poyil Rajeevan*